WINGS TO CHANGE THE WORLD

How does Pollution Affect Animals
and their Environment?

ACTIVITY BOOK

CLAUDIA COMPAGNUCCI

BALBOA.PRESS
A DIVISION OF HAY HOUSE

Balboa Press books may be ordered through booksellers or by contacting:

Balboa Press
A Division of Hay House
1663 Liberty Drive
Bloomington, IN 47403
www.balboapress.com
1 (877) 407-4847

Because of the dynamic nature of the Internet, any web addresses or links contained in this book may have changed since publication and may no longer be valid. The views expressed in this work are solely those of the author and do not necessarily reflect the views of the publisher, and the publisher hereby disclaims any responsibility for them.

The author of this book does not dispense medical advice or prescribe the use of any technique as a form of treatment for physical, emotional, or medical problems without the advice of a physician, either directly or indirectly. The intent of the author is only to offer information of a general nature to help you in your quest for emotional and spiritual well-being. In the event you use any of the information in this book for yourself, which is your constitutional right, the author and the publisher assume no responsibility for your actions.

Any people depicted in stock imagery provided by Getty Images are models, and such images are being used for illustrative purposes only. Certain stock imagery © Getty Images.

Print information available on the last page.

ISBN: 978-1-9822-5124-6 (sc)
ISBN: 978-1-9822-5125-3 (e)

Balboa Press rev. date: 08/05/2020

This booklet is based on the book "Wings to Change the World". It was written for teachers and students who want to work together and understand in detail its message while doing grammar, language and science related topic exercises. Get ready to enjoy the activities and complete them after you have read each chapter. At the back you will find a glossary and questions on each chapter. Let's get started!

BIRDS

Their Bodies and Abilities

"The great bird will take its first flight, filling the world with amazement and all records with its fame, and it will be eternal glory to the nest where it was born."

Leonardo Da Vinci

ORAL ACTIVITY

- ➤ What do you know about birds? How do they fly?
- ➤ Are there any birds that cannot fly?
- ➤ Where do they live?
- ➤ How do birds build their nests?
- ➤ What is a migratory bird?
- ➤ Do all the birds migrate?
- ➤ Which birds do you know that are big?
- ➤ Can you mention a tiny bird?

CHAPTERS 1 and 2
"Wind, the ovenbird" "Ray, the swallow"
GRAMMAR

➤ **Complete the sentences with the correct verb in past tense.**

BE- LOVE- SINK- TAKE- HAVE- BE- USE- START
DESTROY- COMMENT- SPEND-
AFFIRM- SLIP- BE- RUN

1- Wind ....flying and building mud houses.

2- One day he .... an idea. He ....
planning to be a swallow.

3- One of the most important lessons of teaching is to be
humble," .... Wind.

4- The worm .... its chance and ....
through the mud back into the earth.

5- Wind .... disappointed, he had lost his lunch.

6- The Exxon Valdez,..................... and...................... everything around.

7- Sea otters...................... a lot of time in the water, diving and searching for food.

8- He afterwards.............................. the small rock again to open the shellfish,................................ Ray.

9- The slide .... muddy and their light bodies.................... fastly along the way and into the sea.

10- The otters .... splashing foam to one another.

MY WEB ABOUT WIND

> ➢ Look at the following web. Think of all the
> information related to Wind in the story.

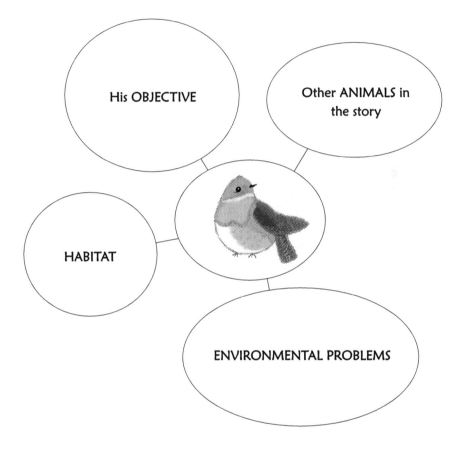

His OBJECTIVE

Other ANIMALS in the story

HABITAT

ENVIRONMENTAL PROBLEMS

MY WEB ABOUT WIND

➢ Look at the following web.
➢ Make your own web about Wind- you can continue adding information as you read onto the next chapters.

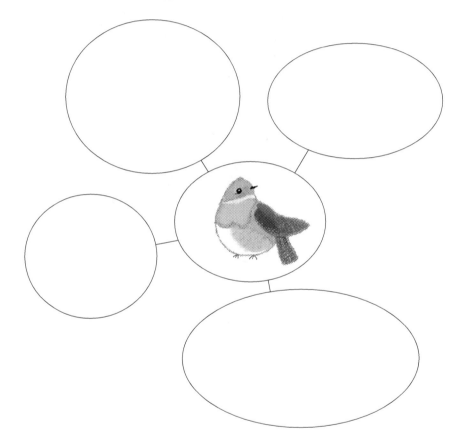

BIRDS PERSPECTIVE

➢ Read the following phrase from chapter two and answer the question:

"We all need to look at life with different eyes. We must look at everything from the heart," explained Ray. "I think they do it because they cannot see it from our point of view."

➢ According to what you have read in chapter two... What did Ray mean?

_____

_____

_____

_____

_____

_____

THE EXXON VALDEZ

➢ **Investigate about the Exxon Valdez.**
➢ **Think about the following aspects:**

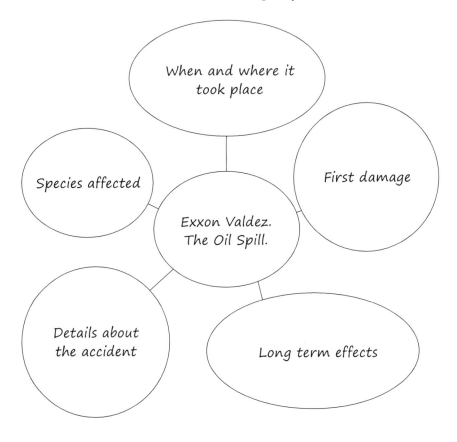

EXXON VALDEZ– The oil spill

➢ Investigate about the Exxon Valdez (continued)
➢ Complete with the information you have collected.

A. Where and when it took place.

_____

B. Details about the accident.

_____

_____

_____

C. First Damage.

_____

_____

_____

D. Species affected.

_____

_____

E. Long term effects.

_____

_____

_____

VOCABULARY

➢ Select the correct word to complete each sentence.

DINOFLAGELATES / KELP ECOSYSTEMS /

HERVIBORES / GENERATIONS /BIOLUMINISCENT /

CARBON DIOXIDE / TRANSPORTER SHIPS
---

1. For …………………………… we have seen the sea shores, mountains, deserts, jungles and rivers from another point of view.
2. The balance of the near-shore is maintained by the……………………
3. Massive environmental damage is caused due to the fact that huge ………………………………………………… sink and spread oil.
4. At night, the sea shore was bright. ………………………………… waves of foam sparkled glow.
5. The mysterious glow was made by tiny organisms called…………………………………
6. They are ………………………………… They like eating plants.
7. Otters can help to reduce levels of atmospheric ………………………………………… which is a greenhouse gas.

CHAPTER 2
"Ray, the swallow"
THE EXXON VALDEZ

➤ Comparing habitats before and after the spill.
➤ According to what you have investigated, fill in the columns with accurate information <u>about the actual spill</u>.

HABITAT BEFORE the oil spill	HABITAT AFTER the oil spill

CHAPTER 3
"Otti, the otter"
THE EXXON VALDEZ

> ➤ Comparing habitats before and after the spill.
> ➤ Read chapter three and answer the questions please:

A.How did the sea otters enjoy nature before the spill? (chapter 2)

_____

_____

B.What happened to Otti´s grandpa when the oil spread in the coasts of Alaska?

_____

_____

C.What did More, the beaver, do in order to help him?

_____

_____

D.What had happened? How many liters of crude oil was the ship transporting?

_____

_____

E.According to what More had read, which products humans depend on derive from oil?

_____

_____

CHAPTER 4
"Fast, the giant tortoise"
THE GALAPAGOS ISLANDS

➢ Identify the main aspects included in this chapter.
➢ Recognize the importance of taking care of nature.

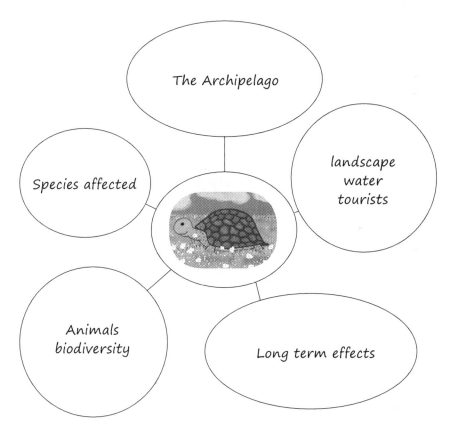

The Archipelago

Species affected

landscape
water
tourists

Animals
biodiversity

Long term effects

CHAPTER 4
THE GALAPAGOS ISLANDS

➤ Identify the main aspects included in this chapter (continued)
➤ Fill in the web accordingly.

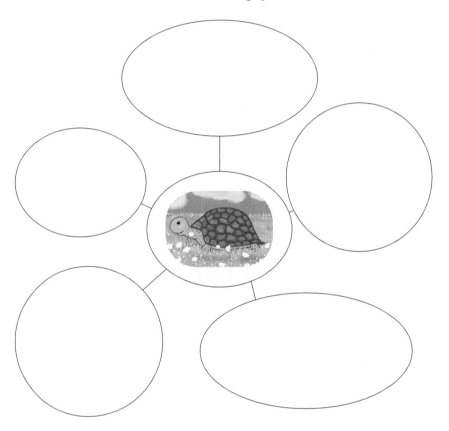

CHAPTER 4
THE GALAPAGOS ISLANDS

The different environments are called HABITATS. Animals can find shelter and food to survive there. Some of the habitats are: rivers, oceans, grasslands, coastlines, mountains, forests and deserts.

> ➤ Identify the correct habitat for each animal, some of them belong to more than one.

Sea lions _____

Killer whales _____

Turtles _____

Tortoises _____

Iguanas _____

Blue-footed boobies _____

Pelicans _____

Albatrosses _____

Masked boobies _____

Sharks _____

Dolphins _____

CHAPTER 5
"Wind builds a new house"
ADJECTIVES

➢ Identify the adjectives used in this chapter.
➢ Choose an adjective for each noun.

Vast - Shallow – Marvellous -
Tiny – Yellow – Sweet -
Comfortable - Bending
Fast – Unusual – Cool -
Overwhelming – Narrow –
Caramel Brown –
Doom-shaped –

1- _____ sticks.
2- _____ branch.
3- _____ waters.
4- _____ apartment.
5- _____ dragonflies.
6- _____ feet.
7- _____ place.
8- _____ countryside.
9- _____ nature.
10- _____ fields of sunflowers.
11- _____ breeze.
12- _____ horses.
13- _____ nectar.
14- _____ roof.
15- _____ entrance.

CHAPTERS 5 and 6
VERBS

➢ Look at the following verbs below.
➢ Identify the animals they are related to.
➢ Make sentences with each one of them.

JUMPING   COOING   CHIRPING   DIGGING   CAWING

SQUAWKING   HOOTING

1- _____

2- _____

3- _____

4- _____

5- _____

6- _____

7- _____

CHAPTER 6
"Sleepy, the sloth"
POACHERS

➤ Read and analyze the following extract from chapter 6.

➤ Identify and Classify ADJECTIVES-VERBS-ADVERBS-PREPOSITIONS and NOUNS writing them in the list below.

-"I want to know the whole story, how did you do it?"

-"Ok, first I will **tell** you how we were caught because that´s the beginning. One **fine** morning, we were enjoying the sun and flying **around** when we **suddenly** heard human voices down in the jungle. The echoe reverberated all **over** the place and many birds **rapidly** flew away **in flocks**. We were shocked to see some men **carrying** guns and some squared sort of boxes which had bars **from** bottom **to** top and all around them. We didn´t know **at** that time, but then we **learnt** men called them **cages**. They were like prisions to keep you **in** forever. At the beginning, I **thought** nothing could happen to us because we were in the **highest** part **of** the **canopy**. A second later, I had changed my mind. I told my wife to stop flying and hide **among** the **leaves** of a palm tree. Our nest was **on** the tree **beside** the one we were hiding in. Apparently, the poachers **had caught** sight of it and wanted to **reach** it. "Oh no!" I thought. My babies **were** inside! I started to panic and began making as much noise as I could to call their attention. In the meantime, one of them **started** climbing **up** the tree. He **must have found** it quite **difficult** for he shouted bad words to his friends **as** he was getting

higher. All of a sudden, a **strong** bumping noise **could be heard** and the **poacher** was on the ground crying out **loud**, complaining **about** having fallen. That was the moment when I felt **relieved.** I thought they **would give up** and leave. To my disappointment and **despair**, he stood up **with** a **quick** movement. He **ordered** the others to bring a **machine** with which they **started cutting** down our **palm** tree. Imagine! They were killing the tree and **wanted** our **nest!** Our babies! My wife started to cry. I screamed **but** my voice could not be heard, for the **deafening** sound of the machine made me dumb. The tree came **down** after some minutes. Those **evil** men **took** our babies **from** the nest. We flew around them to stop them from **stealing** our babies **but** it was **useless.** After a while we were inside a cage as well. Fortunately, they kept us altogether **in** the same **prision,"** said the macaw.

ADJECTIVES

VERBS

ADVERBS

PREPOSITIONS

NOUNS

CHAPTER 6

> ➢ Read the following extract from chapter 6.
> ➢ Discuss in pairs what it means.
> ➢ Write a short paragraph reflecting on what we must do to protect the environment.

-"Oh my! I´m so sorry for you all. It is incredible! These men took them for nothing at all. Now these creatures are dead. And poachers do not have the money they wanted for them. When is man going to understand that we belong to nature?" complained Ray.

-"They will understand when they learn to listen," murmured the macaw.

-"To listen?" asked Ray.

-"Yes, to listen in a different way. To pay attention to little things that are telling them something important. To pay attention to what scientists say. Not only to hear without getting involved. To listen with the heart," added the macaw.

_____

_____

_____

_____

_____

_____

_____

CHAPTER 7
"Mision, the jaguar"

HUMAN IMPACT ON THE ENVIRONMENT

What humans do to nature affects the environment and animal habitats in some way. Planting trees, not polluting the air, not wasting water or not using plastic have a POSITIVE impact on the environment.

BUT BE CAREFUL!

Not taking care of the seas, starting forest fires, polluting streams and rivers or the air, all have a NEGATIVE impact on the environment.

CHAPTER 7
HUMAN IMPACT ON THE ENVIRONMENT

➢ Read the following extract from chapter 7.
➢ Discuss in pairs what it means.
➢ Write a short paragraph reflecting on how dangerous fires can be to nature.

-"Exactly, -*the cloud of death*- I call it. The thing is that I am wondering whose death it will be, for many animals and plants died quickly in that inferno. But man is slowly building humanity destruction through this kind of actions," concluded Mision.

_____

_____

_____

_____

_____

_____

CHAPTER 8
"Freedom the seagull"

THE METULA
➢ Investigate about the METULA.
➢ Think about the following aspects:

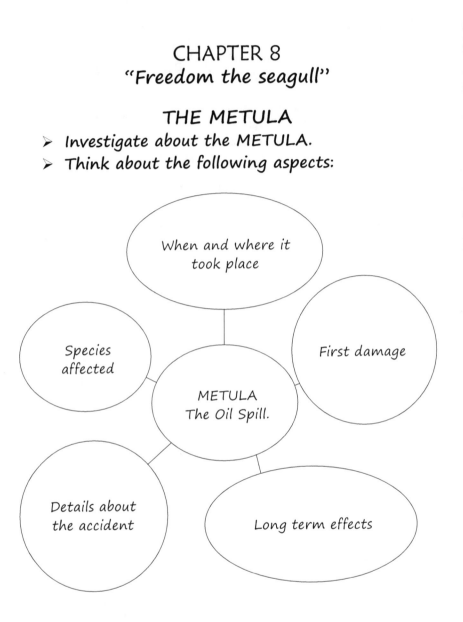

When and where it took place

Species affected

First damage

METULA
The Oil Spill.

Details about the accident

Long term effects

METULA- The oil spill

➢ Investigate about the METULA (continued)
➢ Complete with the information you have collected.

A. Where and when it took place.

_____

B. Details about the accident.

_____

_____

_____

C. First Damage.

_____

_____

_____

D. Species affected.

_____

_____

E. Long term effects.

_____

_____

_____

WRITING

> ➤ Think of the following question and write three paragraphs about it:

How is the pollution we create going to affect us people, in the near future?

_____

_____

_____

_____

_____

_____

_____

_____

_____

_____

_____

_____

_____

_____

_____

_____

_____

_____

_____

CHAPTER 9
"If only men could see"

➢ Read this chapter again and write how the animals organized their team tasks. Which was each one's specific task?

Freedom would _____

_____

Mision and the macaws _____

_____

Sleepy_____

_____

Fast_____

_____

Otti_____

_____

Wind and Ray_____

_____

_____

CHAPTER 10
"Perseverance, the Arctic tern"

➢ Write a summary of the main ideas in this chapter:

_____

_____

_____

_____

_____

_____

_____

_____

_____

_____

_____

_____

_____

_____

_____

_____

_____

_____

_____

_____

GLOSSARY

> Find the meaning of the words in each chapter:

> ## CHAPTER 1

Aerobatics: *noun* loops, rolls, and other feats of spectacular flying performed in one or more aircraft to entertain an audience on the ground.

Pollution: *noun* the presence in or introduction into the environment of a substance which has harmful or poisonous effects.

Migrate: *verb* (of an animal, typically a bird or fish) move from one region or habitat to another according to the seasons.

Environment: *noun* 1. The surroundings or conditions in which a person lives, 2. The natural world, as a whole or in a particular geographical area, especially as affected by human activity.

Wise: *adjective* having or showing experience, knowledge, and good judgement.

Judgement: *noun*: the ability to make considered decisions or come to sensible conclusions.

> ## CHAPTER 2

Generations: *noun* plural noun: generations all of the people born and living at about the same time, regarded collectively.

Oil spill: *noun* an escape of oil into the sea or other body of water.

Transporter ship: a **cargo ship** or freighter is any sort of **ship** or **vessel** that carries **cargo**, goods, and materials from one port to another. Thousands of **cargo** carriers ply the world's seas and oceans each year, handling the bulk of international trade.

Exxon Valdez: The *Exxon Valdez* oil spill occurred in Prince William Sound, Alaska March 24, 1989, when The Exxon Valdez, an oil tanker owned by the Exxon Shiping Company, bound for Long Beach, California, struck Prince William Sound's Blight Reef at 12:04 am local time and spilled 10.8 million US gallons (260,000 bbl; 41,000 m³) of crude oil the next few days. It is considered to be one of the most devastating human-caused environmental disasters.

Perseverant: *adjective* persistent in doing something despite difficulty; unwavering.

Herbivore: *noun* plural noun: herbivores an animal that feeds on plants.

Kelp: *noun* a large brown seaweed that typically has a long, tough stalk with a broad frond divided into strips.

Kelp ecosystems: Kelp forests are underwater areas with a high density of kelp. They are recognized as one of the most productive and dynamic ecosystems on Earth. Smaller areas of anchored kelp are called kelp beds.

Carbon dioxide: *noun* a colourless, odourless gas produced by burning carbon and organic compounds and by respiration. It is naturally present in air (about 0.03 per cent) and is absorbed by plants in photosynthesis.

Greenhouse: *noun* a glass building in which plants that need protection from cold weather are grown.

Bioluminiscent: bioluminescence is the production and emission of light by a living organism. It is a form of chemiluminescence. Bioluminescence occurs widely in marine vertebrates and invertebrates, as well as in some fungi, microorganisms including some bioluminescent bacteria and terrestrial invertebrates such as fireflies.

Dinoflagellates: *noun* BIOLOGY plural noun: dinoflagellates a single-celled organism with two flagella, occurring in large numbers in marine plankton and also found in fresh water. Some produce toxins that can accumulate in shellfish, resulting in poisoning when eaten.

➤ CHAPTER 3

Dense: *adjective* closely compacted in substance.
Struggle: *verb* make forceful or violent efforts to get free of restraint or constriction. *Noun* a forceful or violent effort to get free of restraint or resist attack.
Derivatives: *noun* plural noun: derivatives something which is based on another source.
Strand: *verb* drive or leave (a boat, sailor, or sea creature) aground on a shore.
Magnetic field: magnetic Field. Magnetic fields are produced by electric currents, which can be macroscopic currents in wires, or microscopic currents associated with electrons in atomic orbits. The magnetic field B is defined in terms of force on moving charge in the Lorentz force law.

➤ CHAPTER 4

Archipelago: *noun* an extensive group of islands.
Masked boobies: The masked booby (Sula dactylatra) is a large seabird of the booby family, Sulidae. This species breeds on islands in tropical oceans, except in the eastern Atlantic; in the eastern Pacific it is replaced by the Nazca booby, Sula granti, which was formerly regarded as a subspecies of masked booby.
Whimsical: *adjective* 1.playfully quaint or fanciful, especially in an appealing and amusing way. 2. acting or behaving in a capricious manner.

➤ CHAPTER 5

Cooing: coo *verb* gerund or present participle: **cooing** (of a pigeon or dove) make a soft murmuring sound.

Perseverant: *adjective* persistent in doing something despite difficulty; unwavering.

Dome-shaped: adj having the shape of a dome, curving and somewhat round in shape rather than jagged.

➤ CHAPTER 6

Cawing: caw *verb* gerund or present participle: cawing utter a caw.

Squawking: squawk *verb* gerund or present participle: squawking (of a bird) make a loud, harsh noise.

Hooting: hoot *verb* gerund or present participle: hooting (of an owl) utter a hoot.

Poachers: *noun* plural noun: poachers. 1-one that trespasses or steals. 2-one who kills or takes wild animals (such as game or fish) illegally.

Deforestation: *noun* the clearing of trees, transforming a forest into cleared land.

Canopy: *noun* the uppermost branches of the trees in a forest, forming a more or less continuous layer of foliage.

Black market: *noun* an illegal traffic or trade in officially controlled or scarce commodities.

Captivity: *noun* the condition of being imprisoned or confined.

➤ CHAPTER 7

Flock: *noun* plural noun: flocks a number of birds of one kind feeding, resting, or travelling together.

Macaw: *noun* a large long-tailed parrot with brightly coloured plumage, native to Central and South America.

Perch: *verb* gerund or present participle: perching (of a bird) alight or rest on something.

Reverberate: *verb* (of a loud noise) be repeated several times as an echo.

Deforestation: *noun* the clearing of trees, transforming a forest into cleared land.

➤ CHAPTER 8

Cormorant: *noun* a rather large diving bird with a long neck, long hooked bill, short legs, and mainly dark plumage. It typically breeds on coastal cliffs.

Petrel: *noun* a seabird related to the shearwaters, typically flying far from land.

Albatross: *noun* a very large, chiefly white oceanic bird with long, narrow wings, found mainly in the southern oceans.

Supertanker: *noun* a very large oil tanker.

Strait: *noun* a narrow passage of water connecting two seas or two other large areas of water.

Tidal: *adjective* relating to or affected by tides.

Gale: *noun* a very strong wind.

Preen: *verb* (of a bird) tidy and clean its feathers with its beak.

➤ CHAPTER 9

Boom: *verb* past tense: boomed; past participle: boomed make a loud, deep, resonant sound.

Stricking: *adjective* attracting attention by reason of being unusual, extreme, or prominent.

Generation: *noun* all of the people born and living at about the same time, regarded collectively.

Seagull: *noun* a popular name for a gull.

➤ **CHAPTER 10**

Migration: *noun* seasonal movement of animals from one region to another.

Outcome: *noun* the way a thing turns out; a consequence.

Updraft: *noun* an upward current or draught of air.

Glide: *verb* move with a smooth, quiet continuous motion.

Milkweed: *noun* a herbaceous American plant with milky sap, some kinds of which attract butterflies or yield a variety of useful products.

READER'S GUIDE

➢ **CHAPTER 1**

1. What type of bird was Wind?

_____

2. What did he mostly like doing?

_____

3. Why did Wind want to be a swallow?

_____

4. What is the Earth getting spoiled by?

_____

5. Do ovenbirds migrate?

_____

➤ CHAPTER 2

1. What was Wind doing when Violet saw Ray?

_____

2. How frequently did Ray visit Wind?

_____

3. Where did she come from?

_____

4. Why was the smell from the stream disgusting?

_____

5. What was Ray´s opinion about man making an unsafe use of the environment?

_____

_____

6. Can you name the oil transporter ship that had an accident in Alaska?

_____

7. What happened to the otters?

_____

8. Why did the otters spread fluorescent sparkles in the evening?

_____

9. Which was the name of the tiny organisms that made that mysterious glow?

_____

➤ CHAPTER 3

1. Why were some birds struggling to spread their wings?

_____

2. Where did More, the Beaver, live?

_____

3. What does an oil spill cause?

_____

4. What does man use oil for?

_____

5. Can it be replaced by something different?

_____

6. What happened to Ray when she was overflying Central America?

_____

7. Where did the storm carry her?

_____

8. Who found her?

_____

➢ CHAPTER 4

1. What was Fast, the giant tortoise, concerned about?

_____

2. Which was Fast's favourite animal?

_____

3. How many sea lions did Fast see on the shore?

_____

4. How did Fast rescue some of the animals?

_____

5. What did the reserve guard do?

_____

6. Which is the long term risk for the animals after an oil spill?

_____

➢ CHAPTER 5

1. Which characteristic allows a woodpecker to climb trees?

_____

2. Why was perseverance important in order to build a mud house?

_____

3. Which natural elements did Wind use to build his mud house?

_____

4. Was Wind worried about Ray? Why?

_____

➢ CHAPTER 6

1. What did Ray see while flying over the Amazon jungle?

_____

2. What was the name of the sloth?

_____

3. Do sloths like swimming?

_____

4. What had happened to the macaws?

_____

5. What would happen to the world if men continue to deforestate the Amazon jungle?

_____

➢ **CHAPTER 7**

Complete the following sentences with the correspondent missing words:

1. They were_____of swans flying over the canopy.

2. There was a moment when the _____ wanted to rest.

3. She looked at him while_____on a thin branch.

4. All of a sudden, after a moment of silence, the echoe of the macaw´s voice _____ all over the place.

5. If man continues to _____ or hunting without limits we will all become extinct one day soon.

➢ CHAPTER 8

1. What did Freedom. the seagull, promise Wind?

_____

2. What was Freedom doing when Wind and Ray arrived?

_____

3. Give the correct collective noun for each of these animals:
   A_____of foxes.
   A_____of geese.
   A_____of birds.
   A_____of fish.
   A_____of cows.

4. Give the meaning of the following words please:
Supertanker:_____
Strait:_____
Tidal:_____
Gale:_____
Preen:_____

5. What happened to the little fox?

_____

➢ CHAPTER 9

1. Are there people who want to stop the oil spills?

_____

_____

2. Who do Wind and Ray want to tell what´s happening?

_____

3. How can children help to improve this situation?

_____

4. How did the animals divide their tasks in order to organize their project?

_____

_____

➤ CHAPTER 10

1. Which bird performs one of the longest migrations on Earth?

_____

2. Was Wind afraid of crossing the Atlantic Ocean?

_____

3. What would children do to spread the word?

_____

4. Where had the Arctic swans gone before?

_____

5. Monarch butterflies migrate from the Great Lakes in Canada to

_____

6. How long do they travel?

_____

7. Where can they find milweed plants?

_____

8. How did the birds name their team?

_____

ABOUT THE AUTHOR

Claudia Compagnucci has been a bilingual English teacher in Buenos Aires, Argentina for the last thirty years. **She holds a degree in Management of Education USAL.** In 2008, Claudia took a coaching programme course with the talented American author and personal coach Jack Canfield. After that, she studied Organizational Coaching at Universidad del Salvador USAL in Buenos Aires. Her knowledge and experience led her to start helping other people, mostly English teachers and educators who wanted to improve their performances and have a different perspective on their own lives. She had had a book for children in her mind for a long time. So the day came when she wrote *"Wings to Change the World" "America,"* with the aim of reaching the generations of the future and encouraging them to discover a new way to live in a better world. **,taking care of the environment and protecting our planet.** This booklet: **"Wings to Change the World- ACTIVITY BOOK. "How does Pollution Affect the Animals and their Environment",** accompanies the original book and is meant to help teachers and students at schools. Today Claudia reaches many children personally in schools and libraries where she shares readings of her books. She as well enjoys helping people through her writings and coaching courses, giving them the opportunity to find their inner wisdom to help them make progress. Find out more at @claudcomp INSTAGRAM.

Printed in the United States
By Bookmasters